FNS

gic

BOOK

PER

TR/CKS

JON TREMAINE

QED Publishing

Editor: Michael Downey
Designer: Louise Downey
Illustrator: Mark Turner for
       Beehive Illustrations

Copyright © QED Publishing 2010
First published in the UK in 2010 by
QED Publishing
A Quarto Group Company
226 City Road
London EC1V 2TT

www.qed-publishing.co.uk

A catalogue record for this book is available from the
British Library.

ISBN 978 1 84835 444 9

Printed in China

Contents

How can you walk through a small piece of card or make a coin disappear into a magic cone? Or, how can you make an amazing ladder or a stunning tree by using a few pages of a magazine? It's simple. All you need to do to impress your friends is to follow a few simple instructions!

1 **Preparation**

Sometimes you may need to prepare part of the trick before you start your performance.

Putting on a show

Magic is not just about the tricks in your show, it's also about how you present these tricks to your audience. Excellent magic needs excellent presentation! Remember, also, that your audience wants to be entertained as well as be impressed by your magic skills. Why not have a few jokes up your sleeve that you can use at the right moment?

2 **Difficulty rating**

The tricks get harder throughout the book, except on page 32, so each trick has been given a rating. One is the easiest and six is the hardest. The most difficult tricks will take practice to get right, but the results will be worth it!

Boy meets girl

How can you read some writing that is hidden behind your back. Simple! Your sensitive fingertips will do the reading for you!

1

Preparation

• Write the words 'boy' and 'girl' on the postcard in capital letters. The spacing is important, so imagine the card is divided into nine sections. Each of the nine sections should have either 'Boy' or 'Girl' written on it as shown.

BOY	GIRL	BOY
GIRL	BOY	GIRL
BOY	GIRL	BOY

10

③ Props needed...

The props you will need throughout the book.

- Banknotes
- Card
- Coins
- Colour magazine
- Coloured sticky tape
- Coloured tissue paper
- Envelopes

- Glue
- Magic wand
- Newspaper
- Paper bags
- Pencils
- Plain postcards
- Pretend banknotes

- Rubber cement
- Ruler
- Scissors
- Sheets of white paper
- Sticky tape
- Talcum powder
- Writing paper

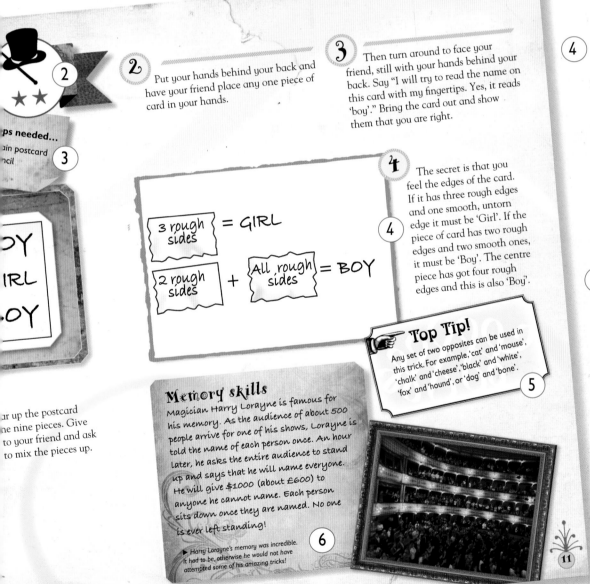

② (top-left: star rating, ★★)

⑨ ps needed...
ain postcard
ncil

② Put your hands behind your back and have your friend place any one piece of card in your hands.

③ Then turn around to face your friend, still with your hands behind your back. Say "I will try to read the name on this card with my fingertips. Yes, it reads 'boy'." Bring the card out and show them that you are right.

3 rough sides = GIRL

2 rough sides + All rough sides = BOY

④ The secret is that you feel the edges of the card. If it has three rough edges and one smooth, untorn edge it must be 'Girl'. If the piece of card has two rough edges and two smooth ones, it must be 'Boy'. The centre piece has got four rough edges and this is also 'Boy'.

☞ **Top Tip!**
Any set of two opposites can be used in this trick. For example, 'cat' and 'mouse', 'chalk' and 'cheese', 'black' and 'white', 'fox' and 'hound', or 'dog' and 'bone'.

ar up the postcard
ne nine pieces. Give
to your friend and ask
to mix the pieces up.

Memory skills
Magician Harry Lorayne is famous for his memory. As the audience of about 500 people arrive for one of his shows, Lorayne is told the name of each person once. An hour later, he asks the entire audience to stand up and says that he will name everyone. He will give $1000 (about £600) to anyone he cannot name. Each person sits down once they are named. No one is ever left standing!

▶ Harry Lorayne's memory was incredible. It had to be, otherwise he would not have attempted some of his amazing tricks!

11

④ Stages and illustrations

Step-by-step instructions, as well as illustrations, will guide you through each trick.

⑤ Top Tip!

Hints and tips help you to perform the tricks better!

⑥ Famous magicians and illusions

Find out who are the most exciting and skilful magicians, and what amazing feats they have performed.

Postcard Magic

Anybody will tell you that it is impossible to make a hole in a small postcard that you can walk through. Nonsense! That is exactly what you will now do!

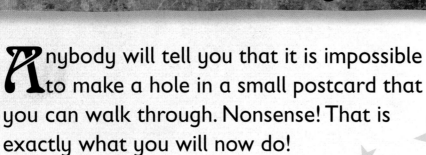

1 Put the card on a table, turn it lengthways and then fold it in half. Press the fold line firmly.

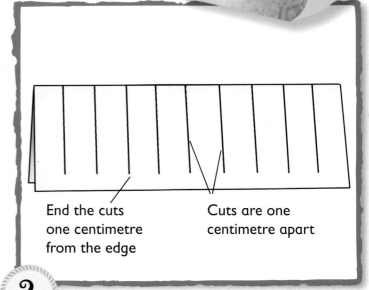

End the cuts one centimetre from the edge

Cuts are one centimetre apart

2 With the scissors, make cuts all along the postcard's folded edge. These cuts should be one centimetre apart. Stop each cut about one centimetre from the outer edge of the postcard.

Second set of cuts along outside edge

3 Make a second set of cuts that start along the outer edge of the folded card. Cut in between the first cuts – stop cutting one centimetre from the fold.

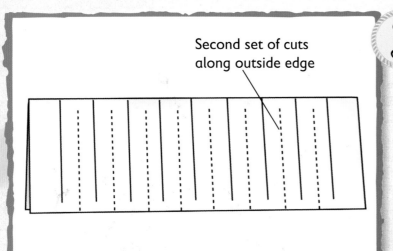

Top Tip!

Why not also try this paper trick with a picture postcard? It will look more colourful and exciting.

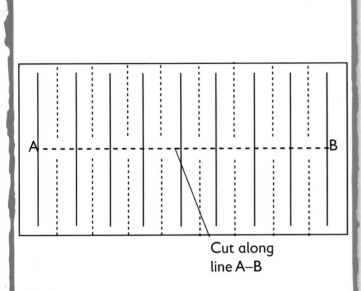

Cut along
line A–B

4 Open up the card and cut exactly along line A–B with the scissors.

Salt Shaker

Dutch magician Fred Kaps (1926–1980) was most famous for a funny trick that he called the 'Salt Shaker'. Firstly, he poured a little salt onto his open hand and closed it. Suddenly, a long stream of salt came flowing out of this hand, which made a mess on the floor. Looking at the audience, Kaps pretended that he could not stop what was happening.

▶ The 'salt shaker' was just one of Fred Kaps' many brilliant illusions. During his life, he was called the 'World's Greatest Magician'.

5 When you have made all the cuts, gently open up the card into a big loop. This will be large enough for you to step through, carefully!

Packets of money

Why not change a small coin into a much more valuable banknote? All you need are six square pieces of paper folded in a special way. The rest is magic!

Props needed…
* Two pieces of paper, each 15 x 15 centimetres
* Two pieces of paper, each 18 x 18 centimetres
* Two pieces of paper, each 21 x 21 centimetres
* Banknote and coin
* Pencil, ruler and glue

Preparation

1. On the two smallest pieces of paper, draw guidelines 4 centimetres from each edge. Then fold the right and left parts into the centre, and the top and bottom parts into the centre.

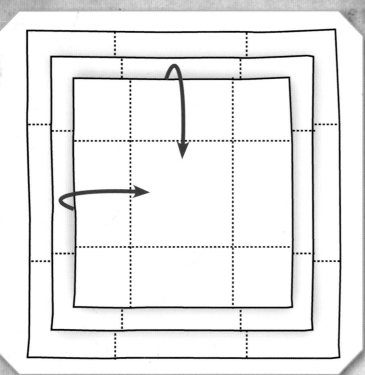

2. Repeat for the medium-sized pieces of paper, with the guidelines 5 centimetres from the edge.

3. Repeat for the large pieces of paper, with the guidelines 6 centimetres from the edge.

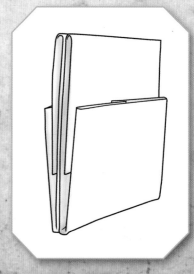

4. Take the two largest folded pieces of paper and stick them together, back to back, with glue.

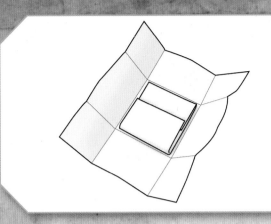

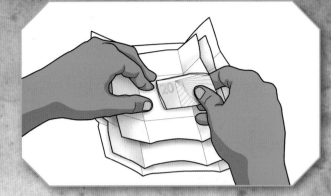

• Put the smallest folded papers inside the middle-sized folded papers. Then, put these combined paper packets inside the largest packets. The packet now looks the same from the front or the back.

• Unfold one side and secretly put a folded banknote in the centre. Refold the paper.

1 Open up the three papers from the side of the packet without the banknote and lay these on the table.

2 Let your audience see you put a small coin on the inside sheet. Then fold everything up again as it was before.

3 While you are pretending to press the folds together firmly, secretly turn the whole package over and lay it down on the table again.

4 Open up the paper and show your audience that the coin has changed into a banknote.

Boy meets girl

★★

How can you read some writing that is hidden behind your back? Simple! Your sensitive fingertips will do the reading for you!

Props needed...
* Plain postcard
* Pencil

Preparation

• Write the words 'Boy' and 'Girl' on the postcard in capital letters. The spacing is important, so imagine the card is divided into nine sections. Each of the nine sections should have either 'Boy' or 'Girl' written on it as shown.

BOY GIRL BOY
GIRL BOY GIRL
BOY GIRL BOY

BOY	GIRL	BOY
GIRL	BOY	GIRL
BOY	GIRL	BOY

1 Tear up the postcard into the nine pieces. Give these to your friend and ask them to mix the pieces up.

Put your hands behind your back and have your friend place any one piece of card in your hands.

Then turn around to face your friend, still with your hands behind your back. Say "I will try to read the name on this card with my fingertips. Yes, it reads 'Boy'." Bring the card out and show them that you are right.

3 rough sides = GIRL

2 rough sides + All rough sides = BOY

4

The secret is that you feel the edges of the card. If it has three rough edges and one smooth, untorn edge it must be 'Girl'. If the piece of card has two rough edges and two smooth ones, it must be 'Boy'. The centre piece has got four rough edges and this is also 'Boy'.

Top Tip!

Any set of two word pairs can be used in this trick. For example, 'cat' and 'mouse', 'chalk' and 'cheese', 'black' and 'white', 'fox' and 'hound', or 'dog' and 'bone'.

Memory skills

Magician Harry Lorayne is famous for his memory. As the 500 or so people in the audience arrive for one of his shows, Lorayne is told the name of each person once. An hour later, he asks the entire audience to stand up and says that he will name everyone. He will give $1000 (about £600) to anyone he cannot name. Each person sits down once they are named. No one is ever left standing!

▶ Harry Lorayne's memory is incredible. It has to be, otherwise he would not attempt some of his amazing tricks!

Topsy-turvy money

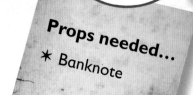

Props needed...
* Banknote

Turn a banknote upside-down just by folding it from side to side. This crafty illusion works every time. Your friends will want to know how it's done!

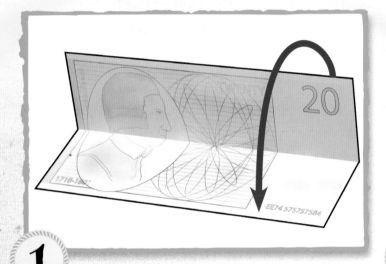

1 Lay the banknote on the table in front of you, lengthways. Then fold the top half down.

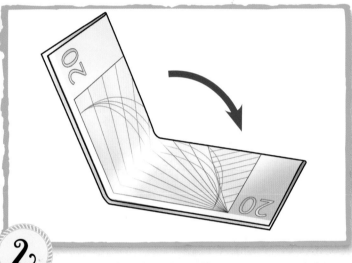

2 Fold the banknote in half again, this time from left to right.

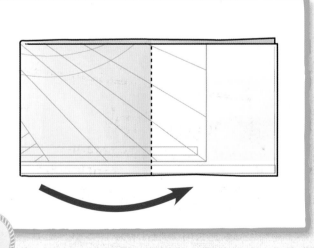

3 Fold the banknote in half, again from left to right.

4 Pull the back fold to the left.

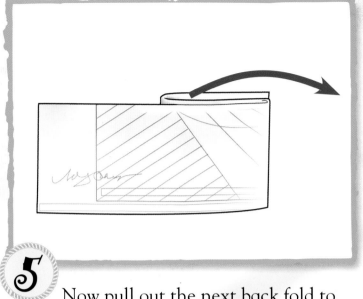

5 Now pull out the next back fold to the right.

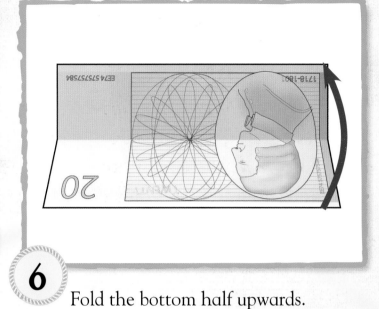

6 Fold the bottom half upwards.

Mr Electric

Magician Marvyn Roy performed a dazzling magic act using only light bulbs. The act was called Mr Electric. In one of these tricks, the magician pulled a never-ending string of glowing miniature light bulbs from his mouth. Later on, his wife leaped out of a gigantic light bulb during a trick called 'Girl in a Light Bulb'!

▶ For over 50 years, Marvyn Roy and his wife Carol Roy performed their light-bulb show around the world.

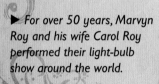

7 Mysteriously, the banknote has turned itself upside down!

Top Tip!

If you don't have a banknote, you can still perform the trick with a photograph that you have cut out from a magazine.

13

Instant tree

Using just a few pages from a magazine, you can make a 3-metre-high paper tree. This looks amazing when you pull it up from a small tube during a magic show!

1

Take the first sheet from the colour magazine and roll it into a tube.

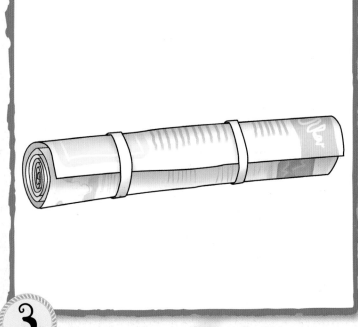

2

Take the second sheet and place it so that it overlaps the end of the first sheet by about 5 centimetres. Continue rolling the tube.

3

Do the same with the next six sheets from the magazine. Put a couple of strips of sticky tape across the last sheet to stop the tube from unrolling.

Top Tip!

Give the tree a small twist each time you pull it out some more. The tree will look more attractive this way.

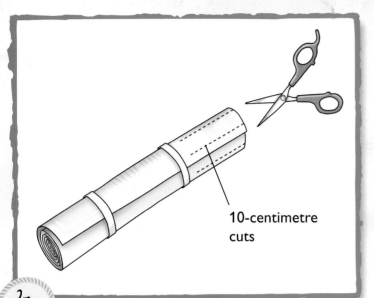

10-centimetre cuts

4 Make a cut about 10 centimetres long in one end of the tube. Then make another five cuts. These cuts should be spaced evenly around the tube. Mark their position with a pencil first.

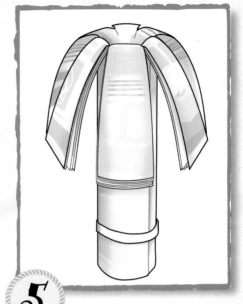

5 Gently fold all of the flaps outwards and downwards.

6 Put your fingers inside the tube and slowly pull out the paper tree. As the tree is tall, you will have to lie it on its side to pull it out. Once you have pulled it as far as it will go, you can stand the tree up.

Shriek of Araby

William Oliver Wallace (1929–2009) was better known by his stage name, Ali Bongo. For his comedy magic act, which he titled the 'Shriek of Araby', he dressed in an oriental costume with gold, curly-toed slippers and a combined fez and turban. One of his best tricks featured a large silver ball that flew around the stage. To make it stop, the magician had to bash it with a mallet!

▶ Before he became a full-time magician, Ali Bongo was manager of the magic department in London's famous Hamleys toy shop.

Raise the ladder

How do you make a long ladder from a few pages of a colour magazine? Simple. All you need is sticky tape and a pair of scissors.

1 Take the first sheet from the colour magazine and roll it into a tube. Take the second sheet and place it so that it overlaps the end of the first sheet by about 5 centimetres. Continue rolling the tube.

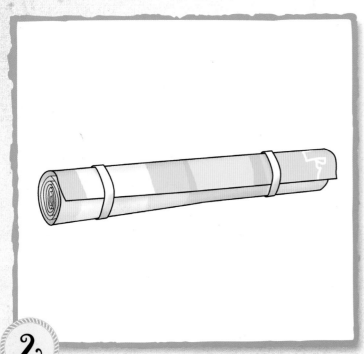

2 After you have rolled the final sheet from the magazine, use sticky tape to stop the sheets from unrolling.

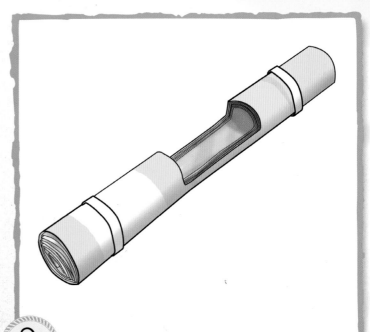

3 Use the scissors to cut out a 10-centimetre-long section from the centre of the tube. Flatten the tube slightly to make it easier for you to cut through the many layers of paper.

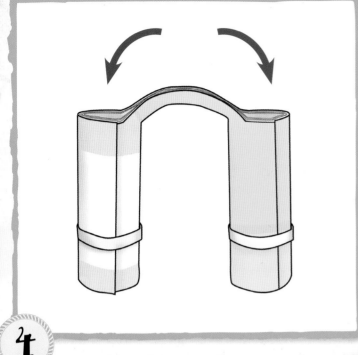

4 Press the tube to make it round again and fold down the two ends.

5 Put your fingers in the centre of each tube and gently pull the paper out. Do this slowly, keeping the two sides even.

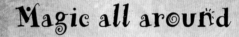

6 Keep pulling the rolled tubes until the paper ladder has been fully formed.

Magic all around

Much-admired Richard 'Cardini' Pitchford (1895–1973) may be the most copied magician of all time. He performed a magical show in which strange things appeared to take place all around him. He pretended that he was as surprised as the audience about this, and that he could not stop what was happening.

◀ *Using simple props, such as billiard balls or playing cards, Cardini captivated his audiences in the world's largest theatres.*

Celebrity spotting

Ask five friends to write down secretly the name of a famous person they would like to be. In this trick, you will tell each friend who they have chosen.

Preparation

• Mark four envelopes with a small pencil dot. Make these dots faint enough so that your friends will not notice them. The place where you put each dot will help you to tell which envelope is which. You do not have to mark the fifth envelope.

• Stack the envelopes in order, with the number one envelope on top. The fifth envelope with no dot is at the bottom.

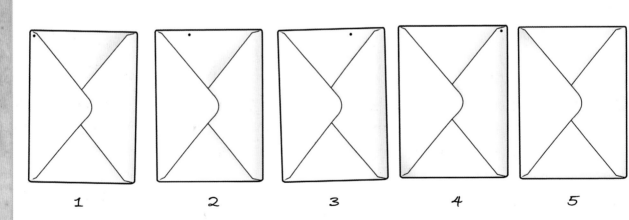

1　　　2　　　3　　　4　　　5

18

1 Hand out the envelopes to five friends in the order in which they are stacked. Give each person a pencil and paper and ask them to write down the name of someone famous they would like to be. Say that they should change their handwriting. Ask them to put the paper in the envelope and seal it.

2 Ask one of your friends to collect the envelopes and shuffle them before giving them back to you.

3 Pick up an envelope and look for your secret mark as you open it. This will tell you whose envelope it is. If 'Barack Obama' is written on the piece of paper, for example, say "Barack Obama, I wonder who thought of him." Look at each person, then put your hand on the correct person's shoulder. "It's got to be you!" Repeat this with the second envelope.

4 Open the third envelope and take out the paper. Let's say it reads 'Robbie Williams'. Tell your three friends that you will do a lie detector test. They must all answer "no" to your question. Hold the slip up in front of each of them in turn and say "Do you want to be Robbie Williams?" You already know whose slip it is by the secret mark on the envelope, so you can pretend to know who is lying when they say "no!"

5 Open the last two envelopes. Read out both names and return the slips to the right person.

Top Tip!
Use your acting skills to make this trick seem complicated. You must make it look as if you are finding it difficult to match the right name with the right person.

Newspaper cuttings

Take a strip of newspaper, fold it over and cut it in half. Then trim a bit more off. When you unfold it, the newspaper is one complete strip again. How is this done?

Props needed...
* Strip of newspaper, 5 x 50 centimetres
* Scissors
* Rubber cement
* Talcum powder

Preparation

• Spread some rubber cement across the centre of the newspaper strip. The cement should cover a patch 5 x 5 centimetres. Let it dry.

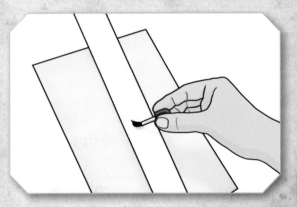

• Sprinkle talcum powder over the cement. Blow away any loose powder.

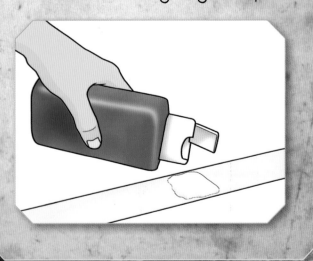

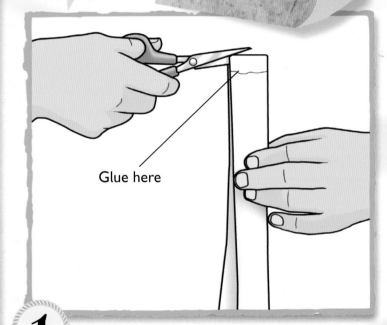

Glue here

1

Fold the newspaper strip in half. The area with rubber cement should be on the outside of the folded strip. Take the scissors and cut the strip in half through the fold in the centre.

Top Tip!

Make sure that the strip of newspaper you use does not have photographs or bold headings. These may make the cuts more obvious to your audience.

2

Show your audience the two strips of newspaper, holding one in each hand.

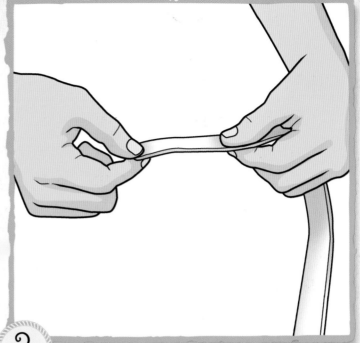

3

Bring the two newspaper strips together. Make sure that the areas you covered with rubber cement are on the inside, pressing against each other.

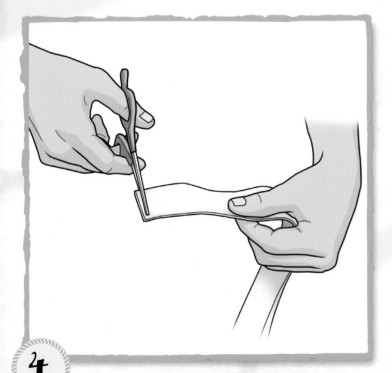

4

Cut off a thin strip, which should be 2 millimetres wide, from the glued ends. This makes the two strips stick together along the cut. The talcum powder stops the rest of the glued patches from sticking to each other.

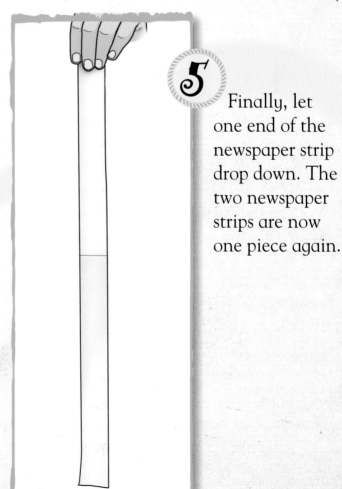

5

Finally, let one end of the newspaper strip drop down. The two newspaper strips are now one piece again.

Magic cone

Put together this clever cone and you can make coins and other small objects vanish into thin air with a wave of your magic wand.

Preparation

• Draw three triangles on the card. These triangles are joined together. The longest sides of the triangles are 25 centimetres long. You can copy the 45 degree angles from this book. Cut out the complete shape. Then draw just a triangle A shape and cut this out as well.

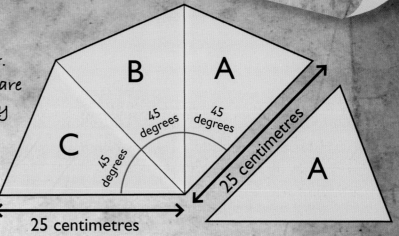

• Put the single triangle A on top of the other triangle A and then stick it down with sticky tape. Do this along the two longest sides. This forms a secret pocket.

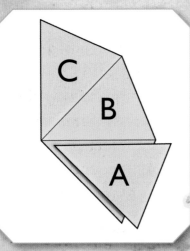

• Put sticky tape along the join between triangles B and C, and along the outside edge of C. Do the same on the other side of the card so that both sides look the same.

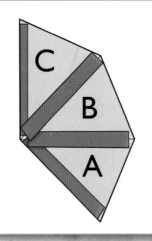

• With the second triangle A on top, fold triangle A over triangle B. Then fold triangle C over triangle B. Press all the folds down firmly.

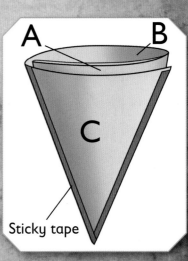

Sticky tape

1 Open up the complete cone and show your friend both sides. Then fold it up again to remake the cone.

2 Gently squeeze the sides of the cone and the secret pocket will open a little. Drop a coin into the secret pocket.

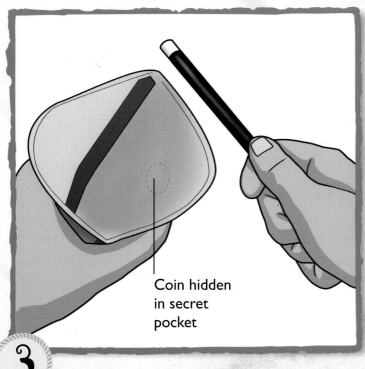

Coin hidden in secret pocket

3 Tap the cone with your magic wand. Open up the cone and show your friend that the coin has vanished.

4 When making the coin come back, first open up the cone and show your friend that it is empty. Then fold in the sides and shake out the coin. Make sure that your friend does not see the opening of the secret pocket.

Top Tip!

You can load all sorts of flat things into your secret pocket. These could include small silk handkerchiefs, folded banknotes, postage stamps or streamers.

White rabbits

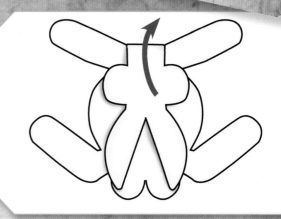

Y ou can also use your magic cone to pull out white rabbits. As you pull out each one, give it to someone in your audience.

Props needed...
* Twenty pieces of white paper, each 10 x 10 centimetres
* Scissors
* Pencil

Preparation

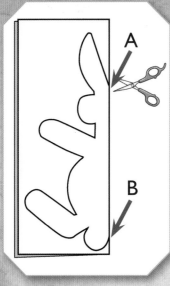

1. Fold a sheet of paper in half and draw the outline of a rabbit. Cut out the rabbit, starting at point A and ending at B.

2. Open up the paper rabbit and fold its head and neck down.

3. Now fold up just the head. Do not fold up the neck.

4. Fold the rabbit in half lengthways and pull its head back a little. Press the creases down and push up the tail.

5. Make twenty rabbits and put them into the magic cone's secret pocket.

Top Tip!
You can decorate each paper rabbit by drawing an eye on each side of the head. This will make the rabbit even more cute!

1 Make sure that you open up the cone and show your audience that the cone is empty. They will not be able to see the rabbits hidden in the secret pocket.

2 Fold in the flaps and wave your magic wand over the cone.

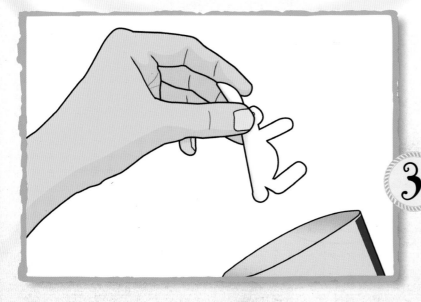

3 Start pulling out the rabbits one at a time. Your friends will be amazed as there seems to be a never-ending line of rabbits for them to keep.

Pick a colour

 Throw lots of small paper balls of different colours into a bag. Ask your friend to take one out and tell them that you know which colour they will choose. You will be right every time!

Props needed...

* Tissue paper in different colours
* Two paper bags of the same size
* Sticky tape
* Scissors
* Writing paper
* Pencil

Preparation

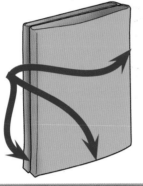

Put tape along three edges

• Use the two paper bags to make a double bag. First, lay one bag over the other. Then, tape them together with sticky tape along the three unopened sides. Magicians call this prop a 'change bag'.

• Make 25 small red paper balls by screwing up small pieces of red tissue paper. Drop these into one side of the double bag. Then make 40 more paper balls in different colours. Ten of these 40 balls should be red. Put these in the other side of the double bag.

I know that you will choose a red ball

• Write 'I know that you will choose a red ball' on a piece of paper. Fold this and put it in your top pocket.

1 Hold the bag so that it is open and your friend can see the opening. Keep closed the secret section containing only red balls. Tell your friend that you will let them reach into the bag to pick out a ball and that you know which colour they will choose.

2 Lift the bag to head height and change your grip so that only the secret section is open. Then roll the top of the bag down two centimetres. This will hide the double opening at the top.

3 Hold the bag up to your friend at head height and ask them to reach in and remove a ball, which they should show you. It will, of course, be red. Put the bag to one side.

4 Then say "There is something I want to show you." Take out the note on which you have written 'I know that you will choose a red ball' from your pocket. Ask your friend to read it and watch the expression on their face!

Top Tip!

You can also make a change bag using see-through bags. As long as you keep the section that contains the red balls towards you during the trick, your friend will not see the second bag. They will only see the balls in the bag nearest to them.

Tear it up

Tear up some tissue paper and roll the pieces into a ball. Then, with a wave of your magic wand, amaze your audience as you fold out the ball and show a complete piece of tissue paper.

Props needed...

* Two pieces of tissue paper of the same colour, both 4 x 5 centimetres in size
* Magic wand

Preparation

• Put your magic wand in your right jacket pocket.

• Lay one tissue paper on a table.

• Crush the other piece of tissue paper into a ball and hide it in your right hand.

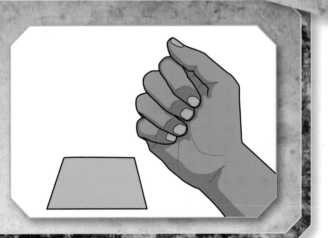

Ball hidden here

1 Pick up the tissue paper on the table with your left hand. Grip it with your right thumb and first finger as well.

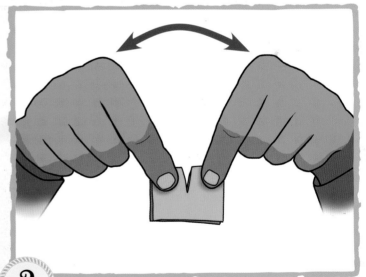

2 Tear the tissue paper in half. Then put one half on top of the other on the table. Turn these halves lengthways and tear them through the centre again. Place all the pieces together and tear them in half again.

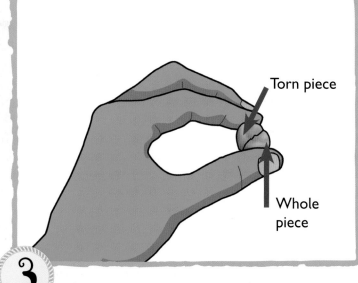

Torn piece

Whole piece

3 Press the torn pieces into your left hand and squash them into a ball. Then secretly push this ball into the ball you have been holding in your right hand. Then hold these between your left thumb and first finger so that they look like one ball.

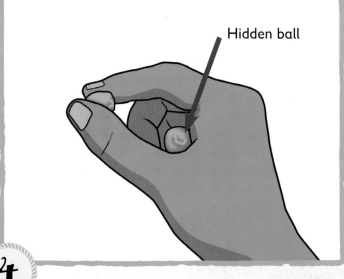

Hidden ball

4 Now take the tissue balls with your right hand. While you do this, turn your right hand a bit. This will help you to hide the ball made of torn pieces behind your second, third and fourth fingers.

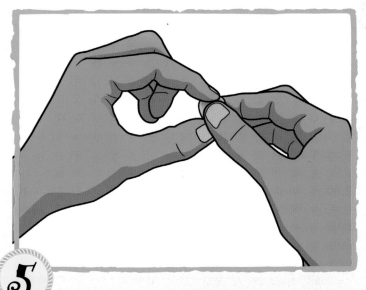

5 Take the untorn ball of tissue paper with your left hand. At the same time, put your right hand in your right jacket pocket and put the torn ball there. Leave the torn pieces in your pocket and bring out your magic wand.

6 Tap the ball of tissue in your hand with the wand. Then fold out the ball to show that it has been magically restored and the tissue paper is no longer torn.

Paper money

Why not amaze your friends by making folded banknotes come tumbling out of a folded sheet of newspaper! All you need to do is to make a secret paper pocket.

Props needed...
* Two identical sheets of newspaper, each with a photograph near the top, right-hand corner. The photograph should be 12 centimetres long by two columns wide
* Pretend banknotes
* Scissors
* Glue

Preparation

• Cut out the photograph from one newspaper sheet. Put a line of glue around three sides and stick it on the same photograph in the other sheet. The open side faces the centre of the newspaper to make a secret pocket.

• Fold lots of the pretend banknotes into quarters and slide them into the secret pocket. Keep everything as flat as possible.

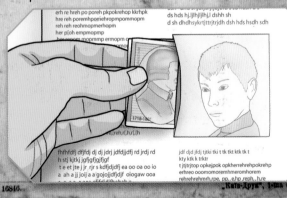

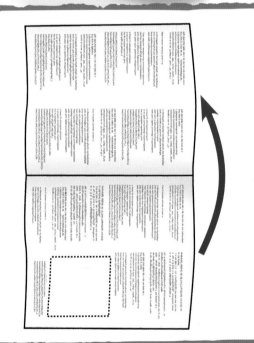

1

Open up the newspaper sheet and lay it on a table. The secret pocket should be facing down in the bottom left corner.

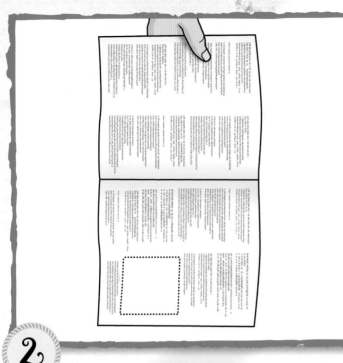

2

Carefully pick up the newspaper sheet by the other end.

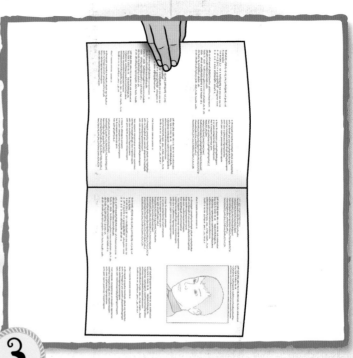

3

Turn the newspaper around to show the other side.

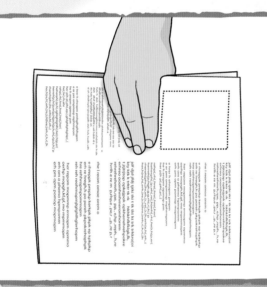

4

Quickly reach down and bring the lower edge of the newspaper to the top. As you do this, the folded banknotes will drop out of the secret pocket and into the centre crease.

5

Tip the banknotes out onto the table with a flourish!

Top Tip!

You could produce lots of other flat things from the newspaper instead of money – for example, postage stamps. If your pocket was big enough, you could even magic a CD from it!

It was an accident!

You will have lots of fun with this popular gag. All you have to do is pick someone who is very proud of their wallpaper!

Props needed...
* Small piece of white or cream coloured paper

Preparation

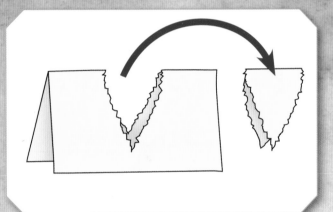

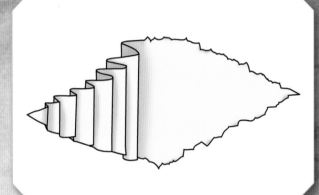

• Fold the paper in half, and tear out a pointed piece as shown.

• Open up the piece you have torn out and put a concertina pleat in one side.

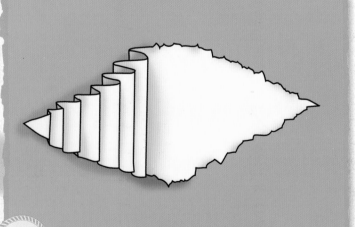

1 Moisten the back of the other side. Then press the piece onto a wall that is decorated with coloured wallpaper.

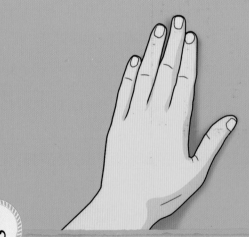

2 It now looks as if the wallpaper has been ripped! Offer to restore the wallpaper by magic. Place your hand over the 'rip', rub the white paper off and all is back to normal.